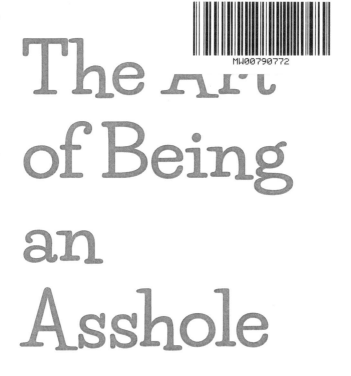

The Art
of Being

an

Asshole

... or not

Other works by Julia Kopala:

When Heaven Comes... Into the Classroom,
How to Reduce Stress and Increase Overall
Well-being Through Holistic Health Practices
ISBN   9-780-98801-420-6

The Art
of Being
an
Asshole

... or not

Julia Kopala

Edmonton, Alberta, Canada

THE ART OF BEING AN ASSHOLE

Copyright © Julia Kopala, 2020

www.juliakopala.ca

Disclaimer:

The content of this book is designed to provide humor and education on the topic of well-being. Most of the suggestions in this book are not to be taken seriously unless they are supporting mental health. This book is a tongue-in-cheek look at asshole behaviour.

Note: the research references, although likely true, are completely fictitious.

The publisher(s) and author disclaim any real or perceived negative consequences or liabilities resulting from the suggestions in this book.

Library and Archives Canada Cataloguing in Publication

Published by Julia Kopala, Edmonton, Canada

ISBN 0-978-0-98801-424-4Paperback
    0-978-1-77354-261-4 ebook

Publication assistance and digital printing in Canada by

PageMaster.ca

Learn from the mistakes of others.
You can't live long enough
To make them all yourself.

— *Eleanor Roosevelt*

Table of Contents

Being an Asshole has Benefits......................... 1

Benefits of being an Asshole 1
How being an Asshole can Benefit Others..........3
Asshole Assessment 4

Being an Asshole to Yourself 5

Asshole Recovery Program for Being an Asshole
to Yourself.. 11

Asshole Baby 13

Asshole Manual for Babies: How to be an
Asshole Baby...15
Encouragement for all parties concerned 23
Asshole Recovery Program for Babies............. 24
Support for Parents of Asshole Babies............. 26

Asshole Child/Teenager 29

Asshole Child... 30

Asshole Teenager 31

Asshole Recovery Program for Asshole
Children/Teenagers.. 34

Asshole Sibling 35

How to be an Asshole Sibling 35

How to be an Adult Asshole Sibling 40

Asshole Recovery Program for Siblings........... 42

Asshole Driver 45

Asshole Passenger - Similar but Different 51

Asshole Recovery Program for Drivers 53

Asshole Recovery Program
for Passengers 54

Asshole in the Workplace 55

How to be an Asshole in the Workplace 55

Asshole Recovery Program for the Workplace, because you want to keep your job, right? 61

The "No Big Deal" Sexual Harassment Asshole. 65

How to be a "No Big Deal" Sexual Harassment Asshole.. 66

Asshole Recovery for the "No Big Deal" Sexual Harasser 72

Support for Victims of the "No Big Deal" Sexual Harassment..73

How to Get the Asshole to Check his or her Own Behavior 75

Asshole Parent 77

How to be an Asshole Parent............................. 78

Asshole Recovery Program for Parents 90

Asshole Guest.. 95

Related but Different... 100

Asshole Recovery for Guests.............................102

Asshole Partner 103

Asshole Recovery for Asshole Partner............ 115

Support for the Partners of Assholes.............. 116

How Not to be an Asshole... 119

How to be Kindergarten Nice. 120

Asshole Recovery Program 123

Confessions of an Asshole........................ 127

Love Letter to an Asshole 130

Author's Note 132

Being an Asshole has Benefits

W hy would you want to be an even bigger asshole than you already are? Well, that is a good question, but an even better question is, why the heck not? Here are some darn good reasons for following the Path of the Asshole.

Benefits of being an Asshole

1 Being an asshole means no one will forget your name.

2   Being an asshole often allows you to have control over others. Kind of like being in charge. It is called power, and power over others works.

3   Being an asshole is your opportunity to pay back the Universe for your sucky life.

4   Being an asshole means there is a 50/50 chance that you will be rich. There are a lot of rich assholes out there. Think about it.

5   Being an asshole is a good place to hide.

Julia Kopala

How being an Asshole can Benefit Others

1 Your asshole behavior gives others something to talk about.

2 Your asshole behavior revs up the listener's metabolism creating better blood flow to the brain. Some research says asshole behavior is just as good as crossword puzzles or Sudoku.

3 Your asshole behavior helps sharpen up the nitwits in the world.

Asshole Assessment

When you are completely sober sit down, one on one or in a small group of your friends. Ask them how you rate as a fine human being on a scale from one to ten. If your friend(s) said you were a 6, would that concern you?

I have never tried this intervention my own self. Bit risky.

The way I see it, you have several options:

- ❏ Remain exactly as you are.
- ❏ Perfect the Art of Being an Asshole.
- ❏ Check out the Asshole Recovery Program.

You always have a choice.

Julia Kopala

Being an Asshole to Yourself

T he Art of Being an Asshole to yourself is rarely promoted by mental health professionals. In fact, being an asshole to yourself is frowned upon. Why is that? What is it they are not telling us?

The following tips on being an asshole to yourself are rock solid and will make you feel like the "piece of shit" you are. My own personal research supports these findings.

1 Start the day by walking into the bathroom, looking in the mirror and saying "I am the biggest loser on the planet." Go on with "what a waste of skin and no one understands me and... hey, is that a pimple!

2 List off all the reasons why your job sucks on your way to work, why the people you work with suck and why you are wasting your life at your sucky place of employment. Recite this list on your daily commute, even if you don't have a job to go to.

3 Learn nothing new. Learning new things just clouds your thinking. You only have so many brain cells. I recommend you do not waste what little you have left.

4 Blame yourself for not being perfect. The more you do this, the better you get at it. Being critical of yourself helps you be the best victim you can be. Many religions are built on this guilt and shame: "through my fault, through my fault, through my most grievous fault."

5 Ruminate about the past. As you age your memory might fade and there is the possibility you might forget some or all the things you have been mad about most of your life. You do not want to lose the focus of your justified anger. Ruminating about the past sharpens your memory. You may even discover something you have forgotten to be pissed about. As you think about shit, more shit will surface – it's the law – shit begets shit.

6 Share intricate details about any illness you may be currently experiencing to anyone who will listen. Big sick or small sick, go deep.

7 Tell yourself every single day that you don't have enough money. In the event someone asks how you are doing. You can respond by saying "well, I don't have enough money."

8   Say to yourself "I've done some pretty
stupid things in my life" and see how
many stupid things you can come up with.
"Well I was really stupid when I..." "I made
a big mess of..." "I really blew that opportunity..." This practice will provide enough
material for your first book.

9   Make a list of everything that is wrong
with your body and then go about the
business of self-correction. Abusing your
body can be fun. You might want to slap
yourself around a bit, especially on the
face so it is easy for others to see the red
marks. It's a good conversation starter.

10 Chew on the inside of your cheeks while
sleeping. Set the intention as you drift
off, "tonight I will chew my cheeks". In
the morning you can get your partner to
check out your "hamburger cheeks". There
is research out there somewhere that
says chewing your cheeks can enhance
intimacy with your partner.

11 Consume mega doses of bread, coffee, pop, alcohol and drugs. This is standard practice for being an asshole to oneself. Skip any form of exercise.

12 Remember it is your job to make everyone happy. Convince yourself that if you just worked hard enough, and prayed hard enough, and tried hard enough you could change people's lives. Of course, this can be heavy burden. What do you have those shoulders for anyway?

13 Watch the most disturbing news/movie you can find before you drift off to sleep at night.

14 Avoid connecting with your old friends. What would the point of that be?

15 Stop smiling. It is a waste of your neurotransmitters.

16 Let the people you live with know how much of a disappointment they are to you.

17 Complain like a professional. Prep yourself by listening to the news and reading the daily paper. Have negative stats at the tip of your tongue so you can dazzle an unwitting stranger at any moment. This will make you look smart.

18 Stop any sweet words from leaving your lips. Giving compliments to others may make you look weak.

19 Frown a lot.

20 Avoid any mental health support. Hope is for sissies who can't cut it.

Asshole Recovery Program for Being an Asshole to Yourself

Is being an asshole to yourself getting you what you want out of life? If your answer is no, consider this brief and/or lifelong recovery program.

Let's look at your asshole behaviour from another perspective; self-destruction is about destroying the self physically, spiritually and emotionally. By your actions you are increasing your level of pain while you are here on this planet. Do you really want to do that?

Perhaps you think you are not good enough or don't deserve a better life; being an asshole to yourself becomes a self-fulfilling prophesy.

Take a moment to consider stopping your self-destructive behaviour.

Ask yourself this question: "would I say or do these destructive words or actions to a small child?"

Probably not.

There is a tender place inside each one of us that is still a small child. It is surprising how few of us remember this. It is our job to look after this little one. Be kind to yourself. There is only one of you.

Know that you are the boss of your own thoughts. Be in charge.

Look around for a bird flying by. Watch the grass grow. Feel a breeze on your face. Be still.

See appendix for resources

There is only one of you...you are enough.

Asshole Baby

Let me be perfectly clear: the word "asshole" and "baby" should never appear in the same sentence.

Recently I gasped in horror when I heard someone call a baby an asshole. "How could you say such a thing?" I screamed in my head. I almost said, "Hey! That's not funny!" And "shame on you!"

And then I realized calling a baby an asshole was kind of funny in a pathetic sort of way.

And then I thought, well, why couldn't a baby be an asshole? What if they had an agenda that unwitting parents knew nothing about?

And then I speculated, what if an Asshole Manual for Babies actually existed and our wee ones were schooled in how to be an asshole baby before they came here? What if the wee ones know more than their parents? What if they already know how to read and they are just pretending that they can't?

Here is my rendition of what this Asshole Manual for Babies might look like.

Asshole Manual for Babies: How to be an Asshole Baby

The most important thing as a newborn, is to remember that you have come on this planet Earth for a reason and that reason is to be your parents' teacher. This is a big responsibility. Your parents will only realize much later in life the lessons you have taught them, so be prepared for some push back from your parents because they will try to control your behaviour.

WARNING TO BABIES: Know your parents' breaking point. Take it easy on them for they do not know what they do not know.

In the meantime, you have some duties to perform.

Crying is a pretty basic requirement for all babies. You know, you cry when you are wet, when you are hungry, when you are tired, when you have a tummy ache etc. But what about good old fashioned "clear those lungs out crying" even after all your needs have been supposedly met? You know – the kind of crying that makes your parents question their decision to have children.

Do you want to trick your parents big time? We recommend that when you are born, come in real quiet, maybe utter only a tiny whimper here and there.

After a couple of weeks of your parents' being in total bliss, you need to drop the good baby disguise. It is ok to "let'er rip". Even though you love your parents, remember they are the adults and they should know how to fix everything, including your crying.

Julia Kopala

2 Once your parents adjust to your new vocal status, change your routine up a bit. For example, cry for 3 days straight, then stop, completely, for maybe 24 hours. You will have your parents tiptoeing around the house in total disbelief with unencumbered smiles.

3 They may even start thinking they can handle this parenting thing. Push the refresh button on your crying spells. Repeat this routine of crying, not crying, but change up the intervals. That way your parents will never be quite sure if they can leave you alone with a babysitter.

4 Whether you are bottle fed or "dine on the house white", have difficulty latching. This is one of your first duties as an asshole baby. Pretend you don't know what your mother is trying to do to you when she attempts to feed you from her own breast. Flail about and screech a bit as if your mother doesn't know she is smothering you.

5 To top it off, all this flailing about is making you hungry and angry. This is the time to roar because you are soooo "hangry!"

6 Sleep is overrated for parents. Your parents can sleep when they are dead. Wake them up and get some attention thus giving them something to talk about to their friends, if they still have any.

7   Refuse to be toilet trained. Just poop all over the place for as long as you like. Poop in your diaper (of course) and poop outside of your diaper where your poop eases down your leg while you sport a big smile. If you are male, take good aim and urinate right on your mom or dad just when they are bending over to tell you how great you are.

8   What is really cool is if you can manage to step into your own poop with bare feet and then throw up on top of it. This takes coordination and exquisite timing.

9   When toilet training rears its ugly head, don't fall for that big girl/boy panties/underwear trick. You have the rest of your life to wear adult underwear. Take your own sweet time in this transition.

10 If a new sibling comes along before you are a teenager, ignore your new sibling completely, but first, cry night and day for a week, pout, shout, puke, kick, and let that lower lip descend to your chest complementing your bouts of refusing to breathe.

11 You are not going down easily because this being the only child is a good gig. Cry so much that your parents, even though it's too late, are second guessing their decision to have another baby.

12 The good news is, in the future you can tell your younger sibling that they are adopted.

13 If your parents or one parent has gone away on business or a mini vacation, refuse to look at them when they come back home. They left you, and this calls for a lifetime of resentment on your part. Hang on to this betrayal.

Julia Kopala

14 Upon your mom or dad's return, ignore their attempts to have eye contact or make conversation with you. Don't cry, just silently turn your head away from them. Disengage. This is where your power lies.

15 Do this until their lower lip trembles and you are sure that they have learned their lesson. Your work is done.

16 When a babysitter comes over cry your face off, screech, reach for your parents, plead and whine until your mom and dad leave the house. Keep this behaviour up for a few minutes because your mom and/or dad may come back and peek through the kitchen window to see if you are ok. You do not want them to catch you in a giggle with your babysitter.

17 Remember the more miserable you can make your parents feel before they leave, the sooner they will come back to you.

18 When you are grown up enough to eat soft food, keep in mind that your hair is dry and could use a good conditioner. Really mix it in there.

19 Make sure to bang stuff, throw stuff, puke, pee, poop and holler whenever you notice your parents are looking at each other "that way". They should have gotten that out of their system before you were born. "Come on!" Parents who have next to no sleep should not be making "those eyes" at each other anyway.

This is your opportunity to turn blue.

20 Stay baby-like for as long as you can. It's a good gig.

Encouragement for all parties concerned:

Dear baby, *you have come here to teach your parents how to be good people, to stretch and strengthen, to grow and groan. Thank you.*

Dear parents, *you can handle this parenting thing. Just figure out how you can get some sleep. Thank you for your efforts.*

Asshole Recovery Program for Babies

The Asshole Recovery Program for Babies is designed for babies who no longer want to be assholes. Perhaps in the few months that you have been here on earth, you may have had a change of heart about your current style of behaviour. Or maybe you just want to give your parents a break.

That is all fine and well, but, given your size, you will need outside help in order for you to change your asshole tendencies. The research shows there is a direct correlation between asshole baby behaviour and uninformed parenting.

In all likelihood your mom and/or dad need a tune up on their parenting skills. How are you going to make that happen, you might ask, after all you are just a baby? Well, from my perspective, if you were able to read the Asshole Manual for Babies before you came here, you can follow this simple direction in the Asshole Recovery Program for Babies.

Throw the biggest tantrum you can muster when the whole family is at the doctor's office. Yes, embarrass your parents. You may not want to do this, I know. This procedure is often referred to as "Reverse Tough Love".

Parenting courses/counselling recommendations from your medical team will be immediately forthcoming. Be assured your parents' parenting skills will improve exponentially thus diminishing your asshole proclivity.

Seriously baby, if you are tired of being an asshole, family counselling is the easiest route to go.

Your future depends on you.

Good luck.

Support for Parents of Asshole Babies

Here is my support for struggling parents.

Parenting is the hardest job I have ever had. There were times when I loved being a parent and there were times I wanted to run away. Indeed, in the early years of child rearing I fantasized about breaking my leg so I could go to the hospital and have my meals brought to me and have some adult conversation. I just couldn't get all the sleep I needed. I couldn't eat a meal without being interrupted and I couldn't for the life of me consider having a date with my partner. I was in a daze.

So why have children? For me it was because I was tired of lunches, parties, and chit chat. My partner wanted to have kids, so I thought why the heck not?

Not all of us are parents or want to be parents. Some of us have tried to be parents and are unable to do so. Some of us have lost babies in utero, as newborns, toddlers, teenagers and even adult children.

There are no words for the loss of a child and yet there are many such losses.

Suffice to say I cannot imagine my life without our children. I know full well there is a risk to having children as much as there is a risk to not having children. No matter what choice we make, our hearts will ache at times. We will grieve for our children, born or not, lost or not. Some of us will be content without having children, or we will be somewhere in between.

When our first child died at birth, I did not seek help, rather I burrowed into my pain and hung on. Initially I turned down help. Maybe I thought I didn't deserve to feel better because my body betrayed me. My sister whose four-year-old child died said to me once "the pain lessens after a while." Many years later I eventually did my grief work. I am a different person because of this monumental loss; I am softer, kinder and less prone to judge.

For those of you who have a child(children) your heart will be opened automatically. Resist the temptation to close it when your children disappoint you, because they will. Love them anyway. Love them in spite of your pride. Love them because they need your love. Always. No matter what.

Keep your heart open. Set boundaries. Ask for help when you need it. Have a date night with your partner once a week even if it is to share a bowl of war won ton soup because that is all you can afford.

> *You have come here to teach your parents how to be good people. Thank you.*

Asshole Child/
Teenager

E verything that is wrong with your life has to do with the outside world: your parents, your teachers, your so called friends, even your dog can be responsible for encouraging your asshole behavior because they love you no matter what you do and therefore they are to blame.

Your questionable asshole behaviour is linked to the fight or flight response which is intended to keep you safe. Flight or fight is about survival of the species or maybe it's survival of the fittest. Or maybe that's Darwinism. In either case, there is good science out there to back up your survival antics.

Do not feel guilty for your asshole behaviour towards your parents, it is expected of you. For the most part it will be educational for all parties concerned. Being an asshole is not your fault. It is in your DNA.

If you were the perfect child/teenager, your parents would have nothing to talk about.

Asshole Child

If you are an asshole child, it is most likely because your parents do not know how to be parents yet. Take as much advantage of your situation as you can. Here are just a few things you can do:

1   Ask a parent to video your temper
    tantrums and put them on the internet.
    See how many hits you can get.

2   Tell your parents that you will decide
    when you are ready for bed. That way
    there is no arguing.

3 Saying "please and thank you" can work
   to your advantage. Study this protocol
   and use it only as a last and manipulative
   resort.

4 Never let your parents have an adult conversation because you are cute and should
   always be included. This is especially true
   when your parents have guests.

5   If you hear your mom or dad swear, then
   it is ok for you to swear. Your swearing is
   especially nice when the aunties are over.

6 Refuse to go to kindergarten.

Asshole Teenager

If you are an asshole teenager, know that this
is the best time of your life to pull off your
behaviour. You can still be an asshole when you
are an adult it just takes a little more finesse to
pull it off.

1   Ask your parents to tell you about their teenage years. This gives you some parameters on which to base your own escapades.

2   Learn how to drive as soon as possible. You never know when you will be asked to drive a stolen car someplace. If you are caught and are underage, the penalty will not be harsh. Seriously, get any criminal tendencies out of your system before you are of age.

3   Voice your expectations about what you are entitled to, otherwise your parents will not know how to shop for you.

4   Never confess if you did something wrong like, damage your dad's sports car. The thing is, you may never get caught.

5   Refuse to clean your room, and cry when you are made to vacuum, empty the dishwasher, do your homework, study, get an education, get a job...

6   Live with your parents for as long as you can.

7   Remember the family sofa is your best friend.

Asshole Recovery Program for Asshole Children/Teenagers

If you discover that you have become an asshole, you need to know this; something is troubling you and you do not know how to handle it and so you are reacting in an unhealthy way.

Have a meeting with your parents, an adult you trust or your school counsellor sooner rather than later. Getting entrenched in asshole behaviour is harder to turn around the older you get. Tell someone who will listen that you are miserable, and you do not know how to fix it.

Your parents and/or a significant adult in your life will screw up, that's a given. It is a question of how much they will screw up and what you are going to do about it.

Asking for help is one of the bravest things you can do in life.

Good luck.

Ask for help…you are worth it.

Asshole Sibling

M any of us are lucky enough to have siblings. Siblings can be someone to play with and someone to fight with. Having a sibling is a big opportunity to develop your asshole character.

How to be an Asshole Sibling

1 Tell your younger sibling, if you have one, that they are adopted. It is preferable to do this when they are quite young giving this revelation plenty of time to sink in. Despite the assurances of their parents, your sibling will never be quite sure who their real parents are.

If they are adopted, remind them frequently that their real parents did not want them. And neither do you.

2. Roll the youngest one up in a carpet or quilt, straddle them and let spittle spring from your mouth on to their face.

3. Give your sibling a diary for Christmas. Have your own key cut or at least know where they hide theirs. This makes really good reading and can give you fuel for your next attack.

4. Never have their back against your parents, their friends, their cousins, etc. Your siblings deserve every bit of antagonistic behavior they get. You can add fuel to this by being passive aggressive. Disengage. Visit another planet while your sibling tries to stand up for themselves.

5. If you happen to feel sorry for a sibling once in a while, this is normal. It will pass.

Julia Kopala

6   If your sibling is smarter than you, make sure you are better at something else. Way better.

7   Name calling is always a good default.

8   Judge the hell out of every decision they make, the clothes they wear, the friends they have, or don't have, the partners they have, what their kids do or don't do... It is your job to keep your position of wise counsel secure in the family. They will thank you for it in the end.

9   If you think your sibling is getting more
     attention and more stuff than you are,
     make a big deal out of this. Fair is fair
     and you are not being treated fairly. You
     deserve better. Stand up for yourself
     because your sibling sure as heck won't.
     Even though you do not know the whole
     story you need to get your parents' atten-
     tion. At least they will not think you are a
     push over.

10   Divide your sibling playtime up where
     each of you get to choose what game you
     play together. Always play your game first.
     When it is their turn to play the game they
     chose, run away and lock yourself in your
     bedroom.

11   Hang out with your siblings' friends.
     Sneak around and hide if you have to
     because you will pick up valuable informa-
     tion and information is power.

Julia Kopala

12   If your sibling is younger than you, it is ok to hang out with them as well. This gives you an opportunity to be a "bossy pants".

13   Run away from your sibling when you are hanging out with your cousins at a family gathering. This will give your sibling the fortitude to fend for themselves.

14   Date your siblings' friends when you are older. This is always a good conversation starter.

15   When you are older don't bother yourself with showing up for important events, like birthdays, concerts, graduations and maybe even weddings, especially if you live out of town. Lots of people get married more than once. Time is on your side.

How to be an Adult Asshole Sibling

1   Make a list of all the asshole things you have done to each sibling.

2   Invite your sibling out for lunch. If you have more than one sibling, it is best to do this one on one. Once you have eaten, acknowledge to your sibling every time you have been an asshole to them. Go into detail in case they have forgotten just how bad it was.

3   When you are done say "I am sorry." This apology absolves you for the rest of your life.

4   Asking for forgiveness is overrated. Really, what is the point of it anyway?

Julia Kopala

5   It is because of you, that your sibling has turned out so well. They have somewhat of a backbone now, are more discerning and are usually able to get out there in the world. If your siblings are successful, it is ok to take some personal credit.

6   It is also ok to let them pick up the check.

7   Have a releasing ceremony and burn your list of asshole behavior with your sibling alongside you. You might even want to hold hands while you watch the asshole list turn into dust. A true friendship might arise out of the ashes.

8   Ask your sibling if they would like to go out for lunch again to give them an opportunity to apologize to you for all of their transgressions. Your treat.

9   Your work is done.

Asshole Recovery Program for Siblings

*D*o you ever wish you had a better relationship with your sibling(s)?

If you want to stop being an asshole to your sibling(s) you need to put everything on the table. Clear the air. Cut to the chase and follow the recommended protocol below.

Going into great detail about all the horrible things you did to your sibling is not recommended. After all, they were there and dredging up the details of what you did only brings back the pain.

The most important thing to do is to acknowledge you were an asshole. Admit it to their face. "I was an asshole to you, and I am sorry." Leave it at that.

Do not engage in a diatribe about your transgressions because there is nothing you can say to undo what you did. Asking for forgiveness is questionable practice because it puts this interchange into a whole other realm which is beyond the scope of this book.

The next generation will thank you for cleaning up your mess.

Clear the air. Cut to the Chase.
Pick up the tab.

Julia Kopala

Asshole Driver

With the collective experiences of myself and my circle of drivers and nondrivers, we have strong opinions about how one can get his or her Asshole Driver Wings.

1 Lay on that horn. The horn is an extension of your arm. Use it or lose it. Unlike the masses, you are equipped with special antennae spiking out of your cerebrum in order to keep traffic moving at or above speed.

I find it especially fun to lay on the horn when the car in front of me is stopped at a stop sign. The driver of that car tends to jump a bit when someone behind them toots. By laying on the horn you will have heightened his or her awareness for the whole day.

A stop sign is not a place to meditate. Student drivers are like babies. Have you ever scared a baby? Put that on your bucket list.

2 Butt in. You know those long lineups where two lanes merge into one? The long line is for those drivers who know how to take their turn, something they learned in kindergarten. Good for them. I find if you cruise beside the long line of drivers waiting for their turn someone will let you in. This is called "looking for belly" (the soft vulnerable place).

Send an enthusiastic "thank you" wave otherwise they might think you took advantage of them.

3 Steal that parking spot. You know when you are in a parkade and some schmuck has been waiting for a car to pull out so they can pull in? It is your duty to swoop in and take that spot before the schmuck.

The schmuck needs a bit of a tune up because they have been blocking the movement of traffic while waiting for a spot. This is inconsiderate.

Besides, you have stuff to do.

4 Speed. Not a lot, but definitely over the posted speed limit. I like to do just 6 or 8 km over the posted speed. This causes the speed cops to ponder their next move; pull you over or not.

There is a danger of getting a traffic cop that wants to boost his or her reputation on the force. They are sharp and fast and may bend the rules to their advantage. You will get ticketed because it is a game for them. Going to court to protest a speeding ticket is pricey because you have to pay exorbitant parking downtown where the courthouse is, get a baby-sitter, get time off work, get an upset tummy...

An alternative approach to everyday speeding is reversing at speed from a dead stop. You still might get a ticket, but it is so much more fun.

5   Hitting a car in the parking lot does not count as an accident and it does not have to be reported. After all the other car was not moving. People are so busy these days that they probably will not even notice the crease or teeny tiny dent on their vehicle.

Really, it is no big deal. You may want to check if there are parking lot cameras. If so, you have to give this one a think; to confess or not to confess, that is the question. If you happen to be wearing a hoodie and neither your face nor license plate can be identified, you've got your answer.

Julia Kopala

6   It is ok to bump a jogger if they are
     wearing black. It's winter, it's dark, the
     road conditions are slippery, and this
     jogger has no markers. If you bumped
     them ever so slightly it may knock some
     sense into them. I mean what jogger
     dresses in black in the winter? They might
     even admit it was their own fault for
     heaven's sake.

     Never confess to a misdemeanor. Deny,
     deny, deny.

7   Clipping a cyclist ever so slightly is a no
     no. If there are no witnesses, you have a
     serious choice to make. Do you stop and
     see if the cyclist is ok or do you make
     a getaway before they get up off the
     pavement?

     Bicycles do not belong on the road and
     they do not belong on the sidewalk. Really,
     it's not your fault.

8   Cutting someone off requires precision driving. Your brain is using mathematical calculations, an activity only highly intelligent people can perform. If you have not been told how smart you are more than once in your life, avoid this suggestion.

9   Run a yellow light because that is what they are there for. Yellow lights are not meant for you to slow down and meekly wait for the next green light. Really, you look like "a pussy when you sit and wait".

10   Tailgating is another example of precision driving. This is when you drive as close to the vehicle in front of you as possible. In order to execute this move you really have to know your vehicle's acceleration and breaking capacity. Tailgating is recommended only for sports car drivers although I have seen trucks tailgate with much success.

Tailgate timing can be a bit tricky. Of course, when you want someone to get out of your way, tailgating works very well. You may even want to flash your lights when you are centimeters from their bumper. You are doing a service to the rest of the driving community if you manage to get a few slowpokes off the road.

Asshole Passenger - Similar but Different

Asshole passengers are necessary because we need order on the road and sometimes a driver just can't do it all.

If you are a passenger, you are responsible for delivering instruction at warp speed using your voice, your hands, and your exasperated expressions, and suggesting what turn to take, where to park and how fast to drive. Make sure to tell the driver what the car count is in each lane as he or she pulls up to a red light. Mathematically calculate which lane will move first according to the age and culture of the driver in each vehicle.

As the car passenger, you embody the latest algorithm on the fastest route. This deserves some respect.

Also feel free to reach over the driver and lean on the horn for them. Like I said, they can't do it all.

Asshole Recovery Program for Drivers

*B*eing an asshole driver can take on a life of its own. It can even control you.

Consider the possibility that you are addicted to the chemical rush you get from being an asshole driver and that you need more and more of this chemical to satisfy the pleasure center in your brain.

So what? You may ask.

Well, you need to know that being an asshole driver is not a singular activity even though you may be the only person in your vehicle. Being an asshole driver messes up the energy field of everyone around you. This causes a ripple effect in the lives of your "victims," an effect you have no way of knowing. The ripple effect is not pretty. Think about it.

You may not care at the moment but consider that another asshole driver in town is messing with your friend, your partner, your kids, and your dog's energy field by the way they drive. Do you really want to be part of that?

You may like to think of yourself as an island. You are not.

Asshole Recovery Program for Passengers

*B*eing an asshole passenger is about you being in control of the driver. Wanting to control other people usually goes back to some childhood issues. If you can admit that, you are halfway there. Read. Talk to someone who knows about this stuff. It's big.

You know that you can be just as dangerous as the asshole driver themselves, right?

Turn in your Asshole Driver Wings.

Asshole in the Workplace

Ever had a job? Ever wondered who was the biggest asshole in your workplace? Ever wanted to be a big asshole but were too timid to try? Help is here!

How to be an Asshole in the Workplace

1 Take credit for someone else's ideas/work. You know a good idea when you hear one and if the schlep who shared their idea with you isn't going to take it any further, then it's fair game.

Ignore the look on your co-worker's face when they realize their project has been scooped. This is a lesson they will not forget-thanks to you. The workplace is no cakewalk.

2 Gossiping is a good way to take a break at work. This gives you an opportunity to connect with your colleagues on a deeper level. Whispering, smirking and the rolling of eyes is quite fun. Besides it feels good to act like you are in junior high again.

3 Mildly mock someone else's ideas at a meeting. An audible snicker will do. Roll your eyeballs a tad and put a little dint in your colleague's irritating confidence.

4   Picking on those below you on the ladder
     is called "punching down." This is very
     easy to do especially if you are on the top
     rung. A very simple example is one called
     "Miss Pat Me on the Head." After you have
     spoken to an underling in a corrective
     manner, smile and pat them on the head
     before you walk away.

     Cutting the legs out from someone in a
     condescending way takes skill and will
     command a serious attitude in the work-
     place, not to mention respect.

5   Without following protocol, help yourself
     first to the good stuff: supplies, office
     space, resources etc. Just take what you
     want. You work hard and you need a perk
     every now and then. Love those pink Post
     Its!

     Maybe the custodian will get blamed for
     the missing stock.

6   Make decisions that affect the work environment of others without their input. For example, when he/she walks into work in the morning, maybe they can't find their desk or classroom. Be polite and say, "good morning, oh, your desk is over there" and wave in the general direction.

7   Never publicly support someone if the boss does not. Always fly under the radar.

8   Allow or expect someone to carry more than their share without stepping in or advocating on his or her behalf. Really, if they can't cut it, they need to find a job that is more suitable to their skill set.

9   Come to work when you are sick. Your input is valuable and necessary. Everyone needs you. Your project will be "less than" its full potential if you are not at the helm every minute of every day. Don't think for a minute that someone else can step into your shoes and carry out your vision. It is simply not possible.

Julia Kopala

10 Swearing makes you look strong. There is research out there somewhere that if you swear regularly, you will get taller.

11 Hissy fits and princess behavior on the job will get the attention you deserve. There is a reason you are "overreacting" and that is because you are right. You will get lots of stares with this behavior. If the staff does not know who you are, they will now.

Don't bottle up your aggression. Temper tantrums have been known to contribute to healthy bowel movements of everyone on staff.

12 Crap all over a colleague's initiative. Tell them that their work is the worst thing you have ever read/seen and that you do not want your name attached to their project in any way, shape or form.

Even though they may have asked for your opinion, your brutal honesty will actually save your colleague from public humiliation. He or she may go back to the drawing board or they may quit altogether.

In any case it is best they know that they don't have the right stuff.

Asshole Recovery Program for the Workplace ... because you want to keep your job, right?

- ☐ Make eye contact and say good morning to every colleague.

- ☐ Smile.

- ☐ Say please and thank you.

- ☐ Get familiar with the phrases " I appreciated when you..." " nice work..." "good job... "

- ☐ No side chatter at meetings. Show respect for the presenter.

- ☐ A joke in good taste is almost always appreciated.

- ☐ Bring a snack to share.

- ☐ Publicly acknowledge someone for his or her good work. This may be easier than saying it one-on-one, and it also makes you look good. You might even feel good.

- ☐ Help tidy up the staff room once in a while. Someone's mother or father is pushing that broom in your place of business. Show some respect.

- ☐ Pay your coffee dues ahead of time. Don't make someone try to catch you with your wallet in your hand. Cheap skates don't pay their share. You are better than that.

- ☐ Cleaning up your language opens the door to promotion. If you show respect, you get respect.

  - ° In general, potty mouths are perceived as less intelligent because they can't find big enough words to express their feelings. Check your thesaurus for alternative descriptors.

- ☐ Your workmates are most likely carrying a mortgage, have some health issues, relationship issues, parenting issues. Some of them are trying to make the best of it for everyone. Consider being kind.

Note: Some points have been inspired by "How not to let off steam at the office" by Sharon Schweitzer, International Business Etiquette Expert, author and founder of Access to Culture– <u>Edmonton Journal</u> NP11 September 16, 2017.

> *Be kind....*

Julia Kopala

The "No Big Deal" Sexual Harassment Asshole.

A re you a practicing harasser or just giving it a whimsical thought? "No Big Deal" Sexual Harassment is where it's at. It is the place where you can be a little asshole and usually not get called out because you really did not do anything wrong, did you?

Becoming a "no big deal" sexual harasser is not for the faint of heart. You have to be highly skilled at it or you could go to jail. Still want to try?

Here are some tips on how to get the best bang for your buck.

How to be a "No Big Deal" Sexual Harassment Asshole

When you enter the field of "no big deal" sexual harassment, staring is a good place to start. I recommend that you constantly surveil your territory, and perhaps occasionally linger on one individual now and then. Not too much.

Ease into this practice. Keep your breathing steady and never look away first if this individual happens to catch your stare. Give a slight smile, maybe a nod, then get back to the task at hand, whatever that may be. Play coy. Make up a task to do if you have to.

Gradually increase your linger time in the following days. Let your eyes move around someone's body a tad, just a tad, keep them guessing. That leaves the door open to who knows what.

Practice, practice, practice.

Julia Kopala

Then eventually stare at your co-worker's chest if she is female or his groin if he is male. Don't go full on right away. Just drift around the territory. They want to be "seen" and appreciated and you're the one to do just that.

2   Put your hands on someone as you pass by them. Pretend it is a tight squeeze and say "excuse me" or "hey, sorry" as you saunter off. Savor the thrill of smelling them up close.

As you know they will be watching you from behind, make it your best swagger ever.

The air will be electric.

3   Bone up on your sexist jokes. There is research out there somewhere that says most women and especially men really do like sexist jokes. Your joke is probably the best they've ever heard, so spit it out.

Sexist jokes can catch your co-workers off-guard and that puts you in a position of power. Being top dog ain't a bad place to be. Ease into this position otherwise you may appear asshole-like.

Test the waters with a little sexist joke on the first go around. Make it so minimal that it would be embarrassing for another to make a big deal out of it. No one wants to be considered humorless.

4 Got a migraine headache? Look for an opportunity to pester that special someone to give you a little kiss or a quick blowjob. Your migraine headache will magically disappear. You might even get a real date out of the deal.

A well-known politician once said in his defence "I did not have sexual relations with that woman" after he clearly was in receipt of a BJ. So, the moral of the story is this; there are no morals when "the little head" is doing the thinking. You can still be president.

5   Call someone "frigid" or "gay" when they
     do not want to participate in your sexual
     fantasy of teasing and flirting. Give them
     the "there is obviously something wrong
     with you" line. It is such an old line which
     is still in use because it still works.

6   Block someone's exit from a room after
     you have had an altercation with them,
     especially if they are a person of interest.
     They will think twice about tangling
     with you in the future. Feel the power in
     this small gesture. You may even smell
     something like fear or excitement coming
     from them. Your nose knows. Do this long
     enough to get your olfactory and/or other
     bodily functions on alert.

7   Put your hands on someone's bum as you
     follow him or her up the stairs. Why else
     would they sway those sexy jeans right
     in front of your face? They are dying to
     be touched. At the very least stare, stare,
     stare.

Your target will know.

8

Massage a "friend's" neck without asking permission. It is especially fun to do in a social setting or in the workplace because it makes you look like a hero. How could a co-worker or a friend object to your kind gesture? After all you are just trying to help them relax and not take life so seriously.

Just start the massage as if you were passing them a plate of cookies. It's no big deal.

9

"No" means "no" does not pertain to you. "No" can mean "maybe" or "sort of" or "keep trying". This can be a bit confusing for most perps especially if you are new at this.

You have a better imagination than most. Be innovative. Be brilliant.

10 Never take anyone seriously when they complain about a little sexual harassment, especially if it is a man. Come on, like this is a problem?

Seriously, you will be doing them a favor if you laugh at them. "Why?" you may ask. Because it paves the way for you, the real asshole to continue what you do best. Be a minimalist sexual harasser. Laughing dismantles any future complaining and if you are the boss, your underling will probably keep their nose down and work even harder than they do right now just to stay out of harm's way. It's a win, win.

Asshole Recovery for the "No Big Deal" Sexual Harasser

If you have not been called out yet, simply stop your asshole behaviour.

Go online and educate yourself about why and how someone might develop a proclivity for sexual harassment. Do this before your "no big deal" sexual harassment turns into a big deal sexual harassment where you lose your job, your family, your life.

Sexual harassment is not about sex. It is about power. Some soul searching is in order here.

Support for Victims of the "No Big Deal" Sexual Harassment

S exual harassment in any form is a "no no" and EVERYONE knows that. It is not only an icky social matter it is a legal matter.

Read this before you talk yourself out of your feelings when actually the more you think about it, the more it makes you sick to your stomach.

Perhaps you don't want to make a big deal of it. Perhaps it doesn't really matter in the big picture. Perhaps you are just overreacting. But what about seemingly innocent yet uncomfortable encounters? You know, the ones you are not so sure about? Do you have thoughts similar to this: "Did that really happen?" "Something is not right here because I am uncomfortable over such a silly thing. There must be something wrong with me."

Do not ignore your thoughts and feelings. The "no big deal" sexual harassment will be on your mind or you will bury it and it will show up in other ways: your mood will change; you will get tense if you come in contact with this person again. You might even get physically sick. Little sick. Big sick.

How to Get the Asshole to Check his or her Own Behavior

You have options:

One of the best ways to handle "no big deal" sexual harassment is to use humor.

"Hey, Ms. Hanky Panky, I need you to stop playing silly buggers with me. OK? Cause my girlfriend/wife wants me all to herself. Ha ha."

OR, you could say, "Hey, your hands on my bum breaches my fly zone. No can do."

OR, when in conversation with a colleague who happens to be staring at your bosom, " hey, asshole, they don't talk!"

OR, you could document the heck out of every uncomfortable encounter, including witnesses, and seek advice. **(highly recommended)**

Your body will thank you.

Change before you have to.

Julia Kopala

Asshole Parent

S o, you got some kids, right? Or maybe you are thinking about having kids and want to know just how hard it might be. Well it's damn hard. Best sharpen up your asshole parenting skills before your kids grow up and take you out.

How to be an Asshole Parent

1

Make sure to yell at your kids the first thing in the morning when they get up. This sets the tone for the rest of the day. Yelling is always a good default. Forget about trying to understand what is going on in their little world. They are just kids. What do they know?

Yell at your kids before they go to bed too. Bedtime stories are for sissies and you don't want to raise any sissies. OR, they might get used to story time and expect this ritual every night. Then you will look like a bad parent when you say no.

2

Never let your babies or small children see your private parts. That is just plain disrespectful. If your child tries to sneak a peek at you while you are changing into a swimsuit, shout "Don't look at mommy's private parts. Shame on you!" Shame is one of the strongest tools a parent can use.

Anything to do with sex can be dirty and you don't want your children to get a twisted view of the body. Besides looking at private parts is an adult activity.

3   Report card time is a good opportunity to highlight all of your children's failures. This encourages them be smarter.

Some parenting books recommend that you tell your children what they are doing right. This is silly because it will just confuse them. They know where they screwed up. And they will know you are lying to them if you tell them otherwise. Highlighting your children's best efforts could make them pompous and proud. "Pride goeth before the fall."

You could also throw in a bit of "I am humiliated that you did so poorly... what will the neighbours think?... and grandma will think I am a bad parent and you know that is not true."

4   Once you get your kids to the dinner table you have the best opportunity to help them be better human beings. They are hungry right? So, they will sit there and take a lashing in exchange for food.

Forget about making dinner a pleasant experience for everyone and look at it as an opportunity to tune up your kids. After all it is a challenge to get the whole family together, right?

5   Never smile or clap if you are watching a sporting event your child is in. Taking them to the game is support enough. And when the game is over treat your child to an ice cream or pop if they scored a point.

Never show too much interest in your child's concerts. I find reading a book or using your cell phone at these events is a good middle ground. You are there and you are not there.

Every once in a while, do not show up to an event as promised. This keeps your kids on their toes. You are building their vigilance and resilience to disappointment.

Best they learn that life sucks from someone they trust.

6. Hollering at the referee at your child's sporting event is a good default. This will show your child that you have his or her back and maybe you are the best parent ever.

7. Don't bother attending your teenagers' sporting events. That's what they have friends for.

8. Never waiver your stance on punishment. It is your job to punish your child if they cross the line. How else are they going to learn?

Ask your child what is their favourite thing to do or have in the whole world and then take it away from them for punishment. I know this smacks of betrayal, but you are sharpening up their wits. It will also teach them to keep their dreams to themselves.

Always use the line "it hurts me more than it hurts you" because, well, it's a confusing line to the little ones and it keeps you in a position of power for a while longer. If you are lucky you can get adult children be-holden to you for the rest of their life.

9

Spare the rod and spoil the child. Hitting your child is ok. You are the parent and you know what is best. You might want to wait until they are at least one year old before you started hitting them otherwise, they may not understand.

If your children are fighting, remember to slap them while shouting "how many times have I told you not to fight?" Make sure the slap is auditory for added effect.

The use of corporal punishment is a bit trickier now-a-days so a word of caution.

Julia Kopala

10 Always take the opportunity to embarrass your child in front of their friends. Your child will thank you for helping them understand the power of teasing and bullying.

11 Don't worry about modeling good behavior regarding swearing. Your child knows very well not to swear in front of you or his or her grandparents. After all, you are the parent and swearing is for adults.

12 It is a good idea to denigrate your spouse in front of the kids every once in a while. Let everyone know who the top dog is. Model how to be in charge.

Two parents playing on the same team or presenting a united front is just unrealistic. It doesn't happen, and if it does, it is shaky at best.

Divided parents give the kids a good opportunity to take sides or try and manipulate one parent against another. This builds their political acumen.

13   Don't forget about name calling whenever you have an opportunity. When they are little, use kid language like "stupid" and "dumb" and … When they get older be sure to use more adult language like "bitch" and "asshole".

Throw in the word "always" when you name call. Like "why do you always have to act like a bitch/asshole?" Be proud of yourself because you are helping create their future. They will remember your guidance long after you are gone.

14   If your child makes a card for their grand-parent be sure to check the spelling. Make the necessary corrections in front of your child so they can learn good grammar and how to present themselves to the world.

You do not want your own parent(s) to think your child is stupid. Your children's bad grammar is a reflection on you.

15   Always compare your children to each other. They need to hear how they stack up against their sibling(s) and so does the whole neighborhood. Pick your favourite child and encourage the other(s) to win your favor. Sibling competition builds character. Best to do this in the safety of your own home.

16   Tell your teenager that you do not trust them. Do this regularly. That way they won't try to get away with anything. They will also go underground with their activities, like a spy. Being a spy can be exciting.

17   Make up an interview list for when your children bring their friends over to play. Like: What do your parents do? What area of the city do you live in? Are your parents divorced? Do you go to church? Do you have a part time job? What time is your curfew? Any plans for post-secondary education?

These questions will make them feel welcome in your home.

18 If your teenager comes home late at night, rip into them before they get their shoes off. Don't wait until morning. Startle the hell out of them as soon as they walk in the door. They will never forget how much you care about them.

You may have to get a few pillows and a blanket to camp out at the front or back door so you can leap up as soon as you hear the door open.

19 Scare your kids on a regular basis. Hide behind a chair and jump out at them. Or what is really fun is, wait until they are staring out the living room window in the evening. Quietly go outside, crawl on your stomach to the desired location and jump up banging on the window while making the scariest face you can imagine.

Practice this in front of a mirror first. These scare tactics will ensure your kids know the world is not safe and they will take precautions and not trust anyone, like their parents.

20 Make fun of your teenager in front of their peers. Do this especially in front of his or her potential romantic partner. That way, you can show them you have a sense of humor and you are a fun person to be around.

21 Disregard any depression or anxiety your teenager may display. It is just a phase and there is a good chance they are just trying to get your attention, like when they were little kids. You didn't do anything about it then and it went away, right?

You could put your foot down and tell them to snap out of it. Or try a catchy phrase like "turn that frown upside down."

In any case there are a myriad of ups and downs for a teenager. Let it roll off your back. It's normal so don't give it a second thought. Certainly, your kid's teachers would let you know if your child were suicidal.

22 Do everything for your kids, especially what they are capable of doing for themselves. That way, when they disappoint you, your resentment will be justified because you have spent your entire parenthood giving, giving and more giving.

There is an added advantage of over giving (it depends how you look at it); your child/children will stay close to home base because they will not trust their own capabilities. However, when they are 40, then it might be time that they paid some rent.

23 Scare your kids away from trying out a new adventure. Even if you have investigated and know there are sufficient safety precautions, scare them away. And if they are under 18, just say no. It is that simple.

Your disapproval will keep them safe and
you will sleep better at night. Your kids
will think of you in their future when they
reminisce about an adventure not taken.

24 Second guess every decision your child
makes. You are the one with some life experience. It's got to be good for something.

Asshole Recovery Program for Parents

*M*ost parents feel incompetent at one time or other while raising their children. This is normal. Let's face it, we are incompetent. We may even have been more than incompetent. No book or advice could ever prepare us for what parenting is really like. We can be the best parent on the block and still mess up once in a while.

I have done some of my best work and some of my worst work as a parent. Parenting can be crazy making and joy making.

As a parent if we think we are right all the time, we are wrong. The important thing is to acknowledge this to ourself and to our child or teenager when we have been wrong, and that what we did or said was inappropriate and hurtful. Talk about your own feelings and never judge your child's. Just because they are little it does not mean their feelings are little.

Always point out to your children what they have done right. If you have to talk about their inappro-

priate behavior, do so when you are both calm and ask your child "can you tell me a little bit about what happened when..." Do not judge them. Ask them how they might handle the same situation in the future. Brainstorm ideas together. Get silly if appropriate. This is an opportunity for both of you to lighten up a bit. Your child's transgressions are most likely not the end of the world.

If your child is in the pit of unhappiness for more than two weeks, ask them if they would like to get some help with their current situation. If they say yes, go about the business of finding a good psychologist. Do this right now. Make the appointment. You may never get another chance.

If they say "no," consider going to counselling yourself to learn how to be a better parent. Tell your child just that. They may come around. And if they don't, you will still benefit.

The thing to take into consideration about counselling is that you are teaching your child it is ok to get some help. Model this when they are children and in years to come perhaps counselling for them will be a natural solution to anxiety, depression and/or suicidal thoughts.

Counselling is the best thing we ever did in our own family. Our children had a voice and our sessions gave us a blueprint to craft our family life together. We did not wait until we were in crises. We went for counselling when things were rocky for a while. It is the best money we ever spent. Ask your school counsellor for a good psychologist recommendation. Do your research. This is one decision that could change the trajectory of your family life.

If you don't like coming home to your family, something is wrong. You are unable see the whole picture because you are right in the muck. Being a kid is tough. You are the adult, get some help and fix it.

Your children are watching you more than they are listening to you. Trying to be a good parent is the hardest job I have ever had. Children model what they live with. Step up to the plate and be the best parent you can be. You are helping create your children's future. Make it a good one.

A wise woman once said to me "your child has come into your life to teach you, not the other way around".

Your children are watching you more than they are listening to you.

Julia Kopala

Asshole Guest

Travelling is fun, especially if it is cheap. Here are some staycation tips while bedding down at a relatives or friend's place.

1   Show up at your family/friend's home or vacation spot uninvited.

   Just knock or ring that bell and enjoy the look on your future hosts' faces when they see you standing there all smiley with your suitcase in your hand.

2   Ever heard the old saying "fish and company stink after three days?" Well, that does not apply to you.

You tell good jokes and you are giving your hosts a reason to clean that bathroom, pull those guest sheets out of the closet and do a quick grocery run. Your presence will give them a focus so they can forget about the problems they are currently having in their mediocre life.

3   Never offer to cook because that is insulting to your host. They will think their cooking is not up to snuff. When you walk in the door it is best if you just ask what is on the menu and what time dinner is. Then go for a nap or a walk so you can be all sparkly at the dinner table.

Remember that putting your fork down when you are full is just plain rude if there is still grub on the table. Eat.

Do not insult your guests by buying groceries. You will make them feel like they are poor relatives/friends and that their life sucks. And it does.

Julia Kopala

After dinner if you notice your hosts headed off to Costco or some big store for more groceries ask them to pick you up some underwear because you are running out. This is perfectly acceptable because you hadn't noticed them doing their own laundry where you could have easily tossed in your skivvies.

4. Do not offer to tidy up because this is along the same lines of insulting the cook. Really, their place is clean enough, isn't it? And if it isn't you could say "Gee I'd offer to vacuum but my back has been giving me a bit of trouble lately, I hope you don't mind if I just sit."

Conversely, if the lack of cleanliness in their home is untenable, it is incumbent upon you to bump up the two-star accommodation to four or five stars. You could ask where the vacuum is, a pail, rubber gloves, a facemask and some disinfectant. It is most likely your host is near sighted and their olfactory senses are shot. Be big enough to suffer your back pain and go for a massage after you disinfect their house.

If you absolutely cannot do the cleaning, politely ask your hosts when their cleaning lady was last in. Perhaps it was just an oversight and they forgot to book again.

5   If you have kids, remember it is their holiday too, so loosen up a little when you are visiting. Let them have their boisterous fun. Your host will appreciate the noisy distraction when they are prepping dinner.

6   It is not polite to offer to take your hosts out for dinner because they will think you are being pompous and showy with your money. It is best to put up with their culinary skills and treat yourself to a great restaurant dinner when you are alone and, on your way, out of town.

7 Make sure to tell your hosts if you
are short of supplies, like toothpaste,
shampoo, deodorant, medication etc.
Follow this with a vacant stare.

8 On drinking beer verses scotch; of course,
you prefer fine scotch but leave that bottle
of scotch in the trunk of your car. Drink
their beer instead. You can always pop out
and have a nip before bedtime.

9 It is also ok to have a little confrontation
with your partner in front of your hosts.
You are human after all and this skirmish
will dispel any fantasy they have about
your wedded bliss. Honesty is always best.
That will help them feel better about their
own lack luster marriage.

10 Before you mosey on down the road, don't forget to check their fridge to see if there is anything you can take for a snack, like some of that fine cheese you suggested they buy, an apple, some garlic sausage, and a bagel. This is tantamount to saying, "hey I like your grub." It is a compliment, really.

Related but Different

If you have been invited to a big family event, turn down the invitation right off the bat. This gives others an opportunity to call you, text you, email you about how important it is that you attend this gathering because it would mean so much that relative of yours who is 96.

Stick to your guns; the answer is still no.

There are many reasons you could give for not attending this event; you have a previous commitment; it is not in the budget (this is a good one because you might be offered some travel expenses) or you just don't feel like it.

THEN, and here is the good part: show up at this family event when it is full swing. Just imagine the hoopla when your little sister sees you walk through the door. There will be screaming and hollering "He's/she's here! He/she came!

THEN your family will jump all over you because this is just the best thing that has happened to them. And to you.

Asshole Recovery for Guests

You can do better.

Fish and company stink after 3 days.

Asshole Partner

Having a long-term relationship with someone is no cakewalk. There will be good times and rough times. For those of you with some life experience, you will know that it is unusual for both partners to have equal amounts of fun at the same time. One of you wants more, while the other one has more. This is a reality.

My parent's relationship was unequal in the "having fun" department; my dad had lots of fun, my mother did not. There are certain things one can do to have a larger slice of the fun pie in your relationship. Being an asshole is one of them.

1 Throw your partner under the bus whenever you can. This basically means you do not have their back and your partner becomes the object of some good-natured humor. This works well especially if you have an audience.

In the big picture you are doing your partner a service by "teasing" them in public. Life is tough and learning how to laugh at oneself is a skill that we all need to learn.

2 Argue with your partner in front of the children, or anyone for that matter.

As much as kids do not like hearing their parents argue, you are teaching them how to "hold their own" and that will come in handy no matter what their future circumstances are. Once the house is empty, because everyone is trying to get away from you, at least you will be able to play video games without being nagged to death.

And if your friends are uncomfortable with you and your partner arguing in front of them, well, maybe you need some new friends.

3   Argue with your partner to bring spice into your relationship. You don't even need an audience for this activity. Really, what would you talk about if you didn't find something to argue about? Arguing on a regular basis will actually save your marriage because it keeps you connected, and it brings on a surge of chemical hormones you didn't know you had.

Put away the cards, the backgammon, and the darts. Get face to face with your life mate.

4   Betrayal is the spice of life. It is totally understandable if you have another relationship that you must keep secret because your partner would not understand.

If and when your partner becomes suspicious, question their thinking, their right to inquire and their sense of fun. Deflection is a great tool. Deflect. Deflect. Deflect.

Your betrayal can spark a complacent partner's interest in your relationship. It turns you into a mystery man/woman full of so much intrigue. The research says if you practice betrayal long enough, you actually become better looking.

5 Keeping secrets from your partner is a topic worth considering. Although still in the betrayal category, little secrets, like "I ate your chocolate bar" are considered a misdemeanor.

A good rule of thumb is this: if your partner would not like to hear your secret, (they would want the information but might not enjoy it) tell them anyway.

Julia Kopala

6 Blame your partner (or anyone else) if
   something goes off the rails. You are way
   too clever to take responsibility for any
   fuck ups.

7 Do not pay a proportional share of living
   expenses according to your income level.
   If you earn more money than your partner,
   well, you earn more money than your
   partner. Reminding them who paid for
   what, forces them to get that extra job on
   weekends if they fall short. That way they
   can feel better about themselves for paying
   their 50% of the costs of cohabitating.

   If you were smart enough to keep your net
   worth to yourself right from the start, you
   would not be having a discussion about
   money in the first place.

8
Invite people over or make couple commitments without checking with your partner first. When you bring home surprise guests, it's kind of fun watching your partner scramble trying to grab the socks and underwear off the lampshade etc. Bringing unexpected people for dinner is right up there for getting that old heart pumping.

Don't forget to slip your partner a couple of bucks so they can run to the beer store.

9
Trusting each other in a relationship is overrated. Really, what are the benefits? Show me someone who trusted their partner implicitly and I will show you someone with a broken heart.

Julia Kopala

10   Secretly buy real estate for yourself in another city to build up your own personal portfolio. If this purchase is accidentally discovered during your divorce proceedings, you can say the property was going to be your 25th anniversary present to your spouse.

11   Never ask your partner what their dreams are. It just messes up your thinking. Never tell your partner what your dreams are. They could take those dreams away from you during a spicy argument.

All hopes and dreams are classified and are on a need to know basis.

12   If your drinking or smoking is ever questioned by your partner be indignant beyond belief. Rant on. Make it perfectly clear that you have always been in control of your intake and that you can handle it. You are in charge of your own body.

Alternatively, you could just laugh at the outrageous accusation. Why? Because your partner is wrong. And laughing about something that your partner takes seriously will make them think they might be overreacting. Call your buddies for support if necessary.

Remember the best defense is a good offence.

13 Save your best smiles for your neighbors, your friends, your workmates etc.

If you smile too much at home, your face will get too tired and the research says that you can literally run out of smiles. Or for sure, you will get more wrinkles.

You need to put your smiles where the payback is, and that is out in the community. If you smile too much at home, your partner will just get suspicious.

14　Save your best stories for everyone except your partner. Neither of you are really on the same page anyway so it is best to save your material for someone who truly appreciates your work.

If your partner loves you, they will understand that when you come home after work, you just need to rest and not talk about your day.

15　Telling the truth in a relationship is overrated. Bend your story a bit to prevent possible judgement or the possibility of hurting your partners' feelings. This is called lying with compassion or compassionate lying.

16   Do not support a partner who wants to go to school or start a new business. A change like this can be too big for your relationship to handle and besides you should not be inconvenienced just because your partner wants to try something new. If they are adamant about their selfish adventure, be clear; it is on their time and on their dime.

In the worst-case scenario, your partner may find someone they like better than you once they put themselves out there. This can be risky. This can also be an opportunity.

17   Be jealous. It keeps you youthful.

18   Nag your partner into perfection. Often our spouses do not realize their full potential, and you must show them how they can reach your goals. This is called love.

19   If your partner is sick or injured, they may need a little extra time to make dinner or do the laundry. Politely ask "when is dinner?" Or, "honey, I don't have a clean towel."

If they ask you to go to the store to get some ginger ale because their stomach is upset, I suggest you go windsurfing instead. Your partner's discomfort will pass. Or a friend may overhear this request and walk to the store to get the ginger ale for you. Win, win.

20   Keep your partner out of major decisions. Like "honey, I sold our boat!" or "honey, I just retired!" Any discussion beforehand would just cloud your thinking.

21 If you still have a partner and he/she is not going anywhere anytime soon, there is no need to change your asshole behavior. As long as you can keep your audience, you seem to be having a good gig. This takes skill. Seriously, if you offend your partner too much, they may refuse to go to the next party with you and then who would be your designated driver?

Note: #13 inspired by Maya Angelou

Asshole Recovery for Asshole Partner

If you are serious about not being an asshole to your partner any longer you will need to look at some hard stuff. There are a variety of ways to do that and the least threatening I can think of is to start reading.

You will discover that most assholes are really hurting on some level. A good psychologist is worth their weight in gold. Cheaper than a divorce. Nix drugs to help you feel better unless you have a chemical imbalance in your brain. Alcohol is a depressant. Do your work with a clear mind.

You can do this.

Support for the Partners of Assholes

*I*n the likelihood that your asshole partner will not ever change, you might want to ask yourself a very important question: "do I want to live like this for the rest of my life?"

A very wise psychologist friend once said to me, go for counselling before there is too much hurt in a relationship. Once you have passed the point of no return, you no longer want your relationship whether it is good or bad and no amount of counselling will change that.

One option is for you is to go for counselling yourself if it is unlikely your asshole partner will join you. Or, they might go to counselling a couple of times and then quit. Then you are back to square one.

Here is the thing-this counselling piece is more about what you are going to do, rather than what the asshole may or may not do.

What I like about counselling is that it can help you make a decision that you can live with. Stay in *the relationship and modify your expectations, keep waiting, or leave. Having a trained listener can help you see clearly.*

Is counselling too expensive? Have you fixed your car lately or paid for some repairs on your house? Are you putting the same financial support into your relationship as you are into your stuff?

Pay for a good lawyer when you need one and pay for a good psychologist when you need one. Get steadfast clarity before you make a move.

Making the decision of whether or not to stay in a relationship is the hard part. Once the decision is made the rest is surprisingly easy.

> *A good psychologist is cheaper than a divorce.*

How Not to be
an Asshole...

So here we are at the crossroads: to decide what you want the rest of your life to look like. Do you want to hang on to being an asshole or consider an alternative, and find the rest of who you are. What might the alternative to being an asshole look like?

How to be Kindergarten Nice.

☐ You can start by making eye contact with the person you are talking to. (It is noted that in some cultures eye contact with strangers or elders is considered rude.)

☐ Ask a question like "what have you been up to?"

   ○ Wait for the invitation to talk about yourself.

☐ Avoid starting or participating in a diatribe about what is wrong with this world. We know what is wrong and most of us are trying to keep our head above water. Stop dragging us under.

☐ However, if you have had personal adversity share this adversity with us, minus the details, and remember to find a piece of hope and/or life lesson. We learn through story. And we are constantly trying to make sense of our world.

Julia Kopala

❏ Never interrupt someone else's personal story with your own stuff. Wait until they are finished and perhaps you will have your chance to speak.

❏ Know the difference between laughing at someone and laughing with someone.

○ The victim of a joke may laugh with everyone else but there will be something niggling at their core way back to a childhood issue. Few of us have healed all the hurts from our past.

○ On the flip side laughing at oneself is a sign of good mental health. If you have a good joke, make it about yourself. Show your vulnerability. This is a sign of true strength.

❏ Check your volume. The whole room does not have to hear you, just the person beside you.

☐ Never use your cell phone while you are talking/listening to someone else. Everyone knows that. Pretend you are in a movie theatre or at a conference where you have to turn off your cell phone or you will be ejected.

Asshole Recovery Program

Chances are you do not know if you are a real asshole or you are just on the rim. In any case, assholes are missing out on something very valuable. What, you may ask? Meaning? Connection? The sweet life? Nothing?

If you want something more in your life but do not know what that might be, start with doing a thorough check of your network. Do you hang out with other assholes? A good way to know is to ask yourself this question: do I feel better or worse after I have spent time with them? If the answer is better, you will be ok. If the answer is worse, you are hanging out with assholes.

❑ Hang out with nature more. If you do not have real nature right out your back door, and many of us do not, go to the Muttart Conservatory or the MacLab Theatre in Edmonton.

❐ Take a walk in our extraordinary river valley. Or go online for bird songs, nature views or to check out local nature spots in your own city.

❐ Set the Intention to be more than what you are.

   ° Setting an intention is like turning on your signal light and giving a heads up to the Universe that this is the direction you want to face. Pick a thought and hold a thought. For example, "I intend to see the good in every person I interact with today."

❐ Read about how to be well from self-help books and from spiritual masters past and present.

❒ Take one conscious breath today. Then two tomorrow. Then three the next day. Shut out everything but your breath. In and out. Notice. One to three minutes of conscious breathing a day will change your life. Note: you need to sit or stand still for this to be effective.

❒ Practice gratitude, every day no matter what has happened. For example, "I am grateful I woke up this morning," "I am grateful I have clean water to drink", "I am grateful I am reading this book..."

> *Be kindergarten nice....*

Julia Kopala

Confessions of an Asshole

*W*hen I was a child, we lived in a small two-bedroom house in Delwood, North Edmonton. We were a lower middle-class family that lived off of our garden, farm chickens, fish from Muriel Lake Alberta and wild game provided by my hunter father. All three daughters in our family managed to get an education because of our mother. "Education is never wasted" she would say. Education was my ticket to freedom. I did not really understand this back then.

My mother knew all too well what it was like to have only a small stipend to run a household and provide the necessities of life for her daughters. Because of our modest living, my sisters and I had to work to provide for our own higher education. A *carwash. A meat packing plant. Waitressing. Any kind of work was valued in our family.*

My mother was a slim pretty petite brunette. She walked with a limp from polio suffered when she was a young woman. Although she loved school, she was only able to complete her grade eleven because of the demands of a life on a farm in Saskatchewan in the late 30s.

My life is easy in comparison to my mother's, I have had many opportunities that she did not. As a teenager I took little notice of the contributions my mother made to the family: washing laundry in a wringer washer, planting and harvesting a big garden to feed the family in the winter, putting up storm windows, baking, canning, butchering chickens on a relative's farm, sewing fashionable outfits for her 3 daughters, cleaning other people's houses, sewing a tent in our back yard...

I diminished the value of my mother many times out of ignorance and sometimes on purpose. Although not my gravest offence, the story of the black cardigan is still fresh in my mind.

Julia Kopala

When I was around 12, my mother bought me a black cardigan sweater because I wanted one for a long time. I may even have whined about it, although whining was not encouraged in our household. My mother took the bus downtown and went shopping with her sparse savings and came home with a gift for her youngest child. When she gave it to me, I wasn't in the mood.

"I don't want it" I yelled at her and threw the black cardigan on the couch. I was angry at my mother because my life sucked and she seemed like a good target. Comforted by her eldest daughter, she sat there and cried as I self-righteously stormed out of the room.

Out of ignorance and on purpose, I diminished the value of another human being, my mother.

What I would give to sit down and have a cup of tea with her now.

Love Letter to an Asshole

Dear Asshole,

I am sorry you are an asshole.

If you are a little asshole, we can work with you. If you are a big asshole, you may need to look at your shit with someone who is smarter than you. You have a choice.

Remember that being an asshole is only part of who you are. Check your anatomy for confirmation. You are not your thoughts nor your words because you are more than that. Who you are is underneath your asshole behaviour.

Perhaps you had to build a wall to protect yourself from your mother or father, a friend or partner who didn't want you and thought you were worthless. Walls are necessary at times. Walls keep people out and they also prevent people from coming in.

Do you want to stop hiding?

Point your ship in the direction you want to go and watch the magic happen.

You can do this.

I love you

Author's Note

Dear reader,

When I was a small child, I could spot an asshole in a split second, even if I didn't have the word to describe what I was observing. One of my dad's friends enlightened me with the perfect descriptor – asshole.

From that moment on I was vigilant and judgemental, "there goes another asshole" I would say in my head, or "could you possibly be an even bigger asshole than you already are?"

When I was a bit older, I often played teacher and lined up my dolls (of which I had only one because my mother discouraged that sort of thing) and stuffed toys (not sure where they came from) on chairs in a half circle around me. In the basement of our two-bedroom home in North Edmonton, I stood in front of my green blackboard, with chalk in hand and proceeded

Julia Kopala

to teach my "students" about arithmetic and how to be the best person they could be. My students had voices. They had smiles for me which made me feel like a darn good teacher.

I continue to teach whoever will listen to me. If you have read this book you are now an honorary "stuffie" in my classroom.

Unbeknownst to me, observing asshole behaviour plus my love of teaching became the seeds for this book.

If _The Art of Being an Asshole_ has mysteriously appeared on your desk or your pillow you might want to do some self-reflection.

Appendix

Resources:

- ☐ Mental Health Help Line, 1-877-303-2642, (Alberta) will connect you to the many services that are available in Canada.

- ☐ Free apps for smart phones are frequently launched, for example, Mindshift, Breathe2Relax.

- ☐ Dr. Joe Dispenza has a plethora of books and Youtube videos online. He delves into the science and power behind our thoughts.

- ☐ Go online to check specific resources in mental health available to you in your area.

Acknowledgements

Editors: Justine Celeste

             Pat Darbasie

Readers: Jean Ure

             Jane Warren

Portrait Photographer: Amanda Gallant

Images: Shutterstock

Design: Pagemaster Publishing

Thank you. Thank you. Thank you.

One learns manners
From those who have none.

*– **Author unknown***

For further information and/or book orders
please see my website, www.juliakopala.ca

To order more copies of this book, find books by other
Canadian authors, or make inquiries about publishing your
own book, contact PageMaster at:

PageMaster Publication Services Inc.
11340-120 Street, Edmonton, AB T5G 0W5
books@pagemaster.ca
780-425-9303

catalogue and e-commerce store
PageMasterPublishing.ca/Shop

About the Author

Julia Kopala is a teacher and counsellor who embodies wisdom, humor and grace.

She believes that learning and laughter is the key to hope and happiness. Julia is a Holistic Health Educational Consultant and a Reiki Master.

She is the author of _When Heaven Comes... Into the Classroom_, _how to reduce stress and increase overall well-being through holistic health practices._

Julia Kopala resides in Edmonton with her husband and partner John. Together they have two amazing children, Josh (Anto) and Justine (Jon).